Jackie Mitchell

Baseball Player

Written by Kaye Sharbono

Illustrated by Mimi Powers

MODERN CURRICULUM PRESS

Prog

Lesl
  M
  C

Jimn
  Cu
  Ra
  Al

Rach
  H
  Sc
  Ca

Laliberty,
acher
lley School District
Colorado

holas, Ed. D.
Educational Consultant
nois

Execu
Proje

MOD
An imp
250 Jan
Morrist

Copyr

ISBN 0-8136-5731-8 (Reinforced Binding)   0-8136-5737-7 (Paperback)
Library of Congress Catalog Card Number: 94-077303

10 9 8 7 6 5 4 3 2 1   SP   99 98 97 96 95 94

Dear Reader,

When Jackie Mitchell was born, she was a very small baby. But her parents helped to build her strength through sports.

Jackie worked long and hard to develop her skills. In this book, you will learn how she made baseball history.

For many years Jackie fought for women's rights in sports. Hard work and determination paid off for her. They can make your dreams come true, too.

Your friend,

Kay Sharbono

Jackie Mitchell was a tiny baby
when she was born in 1914. She
weighed only 3¹/₂ pounds. To help
her become stronger, the doctors
told her parents to keep her active.
Jackie grew up to be a wonderful
athlete, outstanding in many sports.

Growing up in Chattanooga, Tennessee, Jackie's favorite sport was baseball. When she was eight years old, she learned some pitching tricks from the great pitcher Dazzy Vance. Jackie was thrilled when Dazzy told her she had "natural talent."

As a teenager, Jackie played baseball for the Engelettes, an all women's team owned by Joe Engel. He was a former pitcher for the Washington Senators.

Jackie never grew tired of practicing her pitching. She eagerly threw pitch after pitch.

Jackie's father, Dr. Joseph Mitchell, coached the Engelettes. Dr. Mitchell proudly watched Jackie strike out many players. Sometimes, she struck out as many as nine players in one game! He said his daughter was "a curve-ball pitcher, not a smoke-ball pitcher." He meant that Jackie could control the ball, not just throw hard.

Joe Engel also owned a professional baseball club for men called the Chattanooga Lookouts. He was interested in Jackie Mitchell. He thought she was a promising southpaw, or left-handed baseball pitcher. Then he had an idea.

Why not sign a contract with Jackie
to play baseball with the Lookouts?
This would be a dream come true for
Jackie and would fill the stands at the
baseball field, too. Jackie could
hardly believe the good news.

When seventeen-year-old Jackie Mitchell joined the Lookouts, she made baseball history. She was only the second woman to play professional baseball.

Joe Engel planned to have Jackie pitch
when the Lookouts played the New York
Yankees. Babe Ruth and Lou Gehrig
played for the Yankees. They were known
as the home-run twins. Jackie had always
dreamed of striking out the great Babe
Ruth. She knew she could do it.

The big day arrived. With the score at 1 to 0 and a runner on first base, Babe Ruth went up to bat. The Lookouts' manager called Jackie to the pitcher's mound. She slowly walked onto the field, thinking about what her father had told her, "Go out there and pitch just like you'd pitch to anybody else." And that is what Jackie did.

Jackie struck out Babe Ruth. She was stunned when the umpire shouted, "Strike three, you're out!" Next up to bat was Lou Gehrig. Jackie was beginning to feel a little more relaxed. She pitched three times, and it was all over. Gehrig was out, too!

The crowd went wild. They stood and cheered Jackie for ten minutes. She had done what the fans had come to see. Her dream had come true.

16

The Lookouts lost the game to the Yankees, 14 to 4. But it didn't matter. Jackie Mitchell was a winner in everyone's eyes that day, April 2, 1931.

19

A few days later, Joe Engel received a letter from the baseball commissioner, Kenesaw Mountain Landis. He had ruled that it would be too hard for a woman to play against men in baseball. Landis had canceled Jackie's contract.

Jackie spent the rest of that season playing for the Engelettes. Her pitching was never stronger. She won many games for her team.

Jackie played baseball for five more years before retiring in 1937 at the age of 23. She then went to work in her father's optometry office in Chattanooga, Tennessee. Later, Jackie married Eugene Gilbert.

Jackie Mitchell believed that women had the skills to play on the same teams as men. She never stopped her fight for women's rights in sports.

In 1987, Jackie Mitchell died at the age of 73. But her spirit lives on in the lives of women athletes. On December 10, 1993, the National Association of Professional Baseball Leagues ruled that women could play against men in minor-league baseball. Jackie Mitchell would have been proud.

Glossary

athlete (ath′ lēt) a person trained in sports

commissioner (kə mish′ə nər) the official head of a professional sport

contract (kän′trakt) an agreement between two or more people

optometry (äp täm′ə trē) the profession of testing the eyes and giving glasses or contact lenses

professional (prō fesh′ə nəl) an activity that is done by skilled people who are paid to do it

About the Author

Kaye Sharbono is a lifelong resident of Mangham, Louisiana. As an elementary school teacher for thirteen years, she developed various ways to help her students gain a love for reading. Coordinating a family literacy program in Louisiana now takes up a lot of her time. Mrs. Sharbono dedicates this book to her children, Chad and Kayla, who are both baseball players and dedicated fans.

About the Illustrator

Mimi Powers graduated from Syracuse University with a degree in Illustration. For the past fifteen years she has been a freelance illustrator. Her work has appeared in several "Highlights for Children" publications as well as in children's textbooks. In *Jackie Mitchell*, Ms. Powers used a combination of airbrush and colored pencils to bring an interesting time in American history to life.